ERNST RÖTTGER # Creative Wood Design

 NEW YORK **Reinhold Publishing Corporation**

© Otto Maier Verlag, Ravensburg, Germany 1960

Published in the United States of America 1961
by Reinhold Publishing Corporation
Library of Congress Catalog Number 61-10979
Printed in the United States of America
by The Guinn Co., Inc. New York
Second Printing 1963
Third Printing 1965

CONTENTS

PREFACE

'The time has now come when any man who cannot turn to some form of art or handicraft is extremely unfortunate. With the world moving at its present pace, mere knowledge avails us nothing; by the time a man has taken note of all there is to know, he has lost his essential self.'

Over a hundred years ago Goethe foresaw the nature of a world that would surely come and would, as surely, result in the malady from which we are now suffering. Scientific and technological concepts, in terms of which we now tend to interpret the world, do nothing to nourish the innate humanity within us; indeed, such concepts must ultimately destroy this quality, for the manner in which we are ordering our lives to an ever increasing degree cannot do other than cause the humanity within us, inspired by abstract ideas, to sicken and wither.

Man loses 'his essential self'—he loses that which makes a human being truly human, the individual quality, the quality that must be nurtured, educated and exercised in order to survive. Goethe said that art and handicrafts are the means for nourishing this inner being. What he had in mind was an activity in which both our senses and our moral faculty participate, an activity involving hand, soul and spirit, each of these contributing its share with an equal degree of intensity. Such an activity is the precise goal of this series; seeking this goal justifies our work.

The educational path described in these volumes is intended to reawaken our ability to take pleasure in creative play. By exercising our creative powers we strengthen and develop our individuality and begin to develop a critical quality of the senses. This helps us to recognize the circumstances of our lives that are out of tune with our humanity, that are in fact inhuman. It also helps us to take a clearly defined attitude towards such matters and thus we learn to free ourselves from their influence. The effect of this kind of learning will extend through the whole of our lives.

Ernst Röttger devotes this, the second volume of his work on Creative Play, to wood—the earliest material used by man for making and building things. Think for a moment of all the things that were made of wood before we began to sacrifice the forests of the earth in order to produce newsprint and packaging material. The catalogue is vast. It ranges from bowls, beds and tables, from wagons, boats and wheels to houses and churches. An infinitely varied experience has been acquired over the ages in the working of this material. With every task this accummulated experience must be considered.

4

Wood is an organic substance. Each kind of wood therefore imposes its own conditions for successful working, and those conditions often vary from one piece of work to another. In every case the conditions must be known and accepted. The characteristics of any material and the varied possibilities of treatment can always in some measure induce that heightened critical quality of the senses referred to previously. But wood requires a more inexorable discipline than any other substance, and its revenge for faulty treatment is not only immediate, it is unrelenting.

Tschuang Tse's story of the wood carver goes to the heart of the matter:

A wood carver once carved a bell-rest. When it was finished, all who beheld it marvelled, considering it a divine piece of work. The Duke of Lu also gazed upon it and questioned the master, saying, 'What is your secret?' To which the wood carver replied, 'I am a man who works with his hands and I have no secrets. And yet there is one thing that is truly needful. When I had made up my mind to carve the bell-rest, I was careful not to expend my energies on thoughts of other things. So that my heart might be at rest, I fasted, and after three days I no longer thought of honours or reward. After five days I no longer thought of praise or blame, and after seven days I had forgotten that I had a body or limbs, nor at that stage had I any longer any thought for Your Highness' court. Thus I became truly serene and could pursue my object with complete singleness of mind, for all disturbing influence from the outer world had disappeared. I then went into the forest and looked at the trees. As soon as I set eyes on the right tree, the bell-rest appeared before me as though finished and I needed only to set my hand to work. Had I not found this tree, I would have abandoned the task. It is because I allowed my own nature to work along with the nature of my material that people now consider this to be a divine piece of work.'

If we can but conceive of our task in such direct and simple terms as these, if in setting about it we have respect for its essential character, then surely at the right moment the right idea will come to us.

Then it may well be that something truly worthwhile will emerge from our serious yet light-hearted play. The spirit and guiding principles are here made plain and some of the results are illustrated. If we follow this guidance something may come into being that, like the Chinese bell-rest, will bring joy to the heart.

Heinrich Lauterbach

INTRODUCTION

One of the most basic aptitudes of man is an ability to create form. In every child there stirs a natural urge to fashion shapes of one kind or another, to paint and to draw. Although the child's first attempts at self-expression show pure creativity, later the lack of adult understanding tends to suppress or divert this natural instinct. Overvaluation of the mental approach and excessive encouragement of the imitative instinct soon lead to the atrophy of all aptitude for spontaneous invention and creation. In addition, we now have mass supply of machine-made products; these rob the child of the pleasure of making things for himself and so make him uncertain of his value judgments.

It is the purpose of this book to suggest and illustrate ways in which the creative urge and the faculty of invention may be reawakened. The illustrations show the results of an activity that has been developed on the principles of play. They show the work of children, of adult amateurs and the first exercises of students.

In work such as this, comprehension by the senses must precede any planning by conscious thought; the world of forms that is conjured up by the imagination must not be allowed to lose its brightness by permitting scientific concepts to impinge upon it. Furthermore, standards must not be set so high that they retard spontaneity, nor should the aim be anything that might properly be called an artistic achievement. The objects represented here have nothing to do with academic art. They are the products of an activity in which anyone can engage, activity of a kind that is as indispensible as food and clothing, if life is to have some kind of content and meaning.

The manner in which these various objects have taken shape should be made clear largely by the illustrations themselves. The short texts are intended to be merely supplementary. Overexact technical directions would only rob the person concerned of the pleasure that can be experienced in finding new ways of giving an object the desired form. The illustrations, therefore, should not be considered as providing models to be copied. They do no more than exhibit the products of certain methods by which an endless variety of results can be achieved.

Cassel, Spring 1960   Ernst Röttger

To the man of the technological age the nature of true play is largely unknown. Today we seem to know only certain kinds of games—those designed for pure diversion and those primarily concerned with achieving outstanding feats and breaking records.

If we wish to see the phenomenon of play in its original form and to understand its original significance, we must seek it in the realm of childhood and in art. In the field of the performing arts we actually use the verb 'to play' when describing the work of a musician. In the sculptural and pictorial arts, however, there is no place for the term. Yet, if we examine the latest developments in these arts, we come upon a method of procedure that has a distinct relationship to the kind of play referred to in this book, that is, play governed by the twin purposes of creation and discovery. For example, the contemporary artist often refuses to subordinate his materials to an idea and, in fact, often starts his work without any clear preconceived plan. He frequently prefers to treat the material as the datum, to proceed in a half-playful, half-serious mood, permitting the material itself to suggest wholly new ideas.

We must, however, distinguish very sharply between play and mere playfulness, between an activity that is essentially creative and one that is nothing more than purposeless trifling. Haphazard practices know no rules and respect no principle of order. They result from a mere urge to be doing something, no matter what, and usually stem from boredom or simply from a natural desire for relaxation and diversion. True play makes demands upon the player and requires him to observe the rules of the game. Creative play differs from ordinary work with physical material in that it is not intended to serve any useful purpose. The nature of the ultimate product is unknown while it is in the making and the point of the activity is the activity itself. Engaged in play of this kind, we find ourselves really discovering the peculiarities of our material, we discern what it is that endows it with its distinctive character, we discover also the right way of employing our tools upon it, and our minds begin to see it in new and original forms. With a sense of delight we begin to experience the reawakening of our creative faculties, which had been deadened by misdirection and preoccupation with imitating and copying.

Our play proceeds under certain broad directives to ensure that our efforts are never wholly without meaning.

These directives determine our choice of materials and, in a general way, the shape that such material is ultimately to assume. They direct our choice of tools and help us divide our play into logical stages. Thus they guide us in an activity that is disciplined and therefore satisfying.

The great variety of creative means is impressive. In addition to tools and the many different materials available for our use, we must also include, as creative means, the constituent elements of design—dots, lines, planes, mass, dimensions, colour—and the basic principles of composition, that is, proportion, rhythm and contrast.

Explanation of symbols:

S = Work of a student of the Staatliche Werkakademie in Cassel

I = From instructional courses for adults and teachers

C = Children's work

The small figures denote the age of the child concerned.

The illustrations in this book are all of objects produced under the tuition of Ernst Röttger and Dieter Klante or during instructional courses given by them.

1

2 S Walnut

Starting with a Block of Wood

SHAPE AND TOUCH

The simplest way to begin our play is to start with an ordinary block of wood. We can use waste from a workshop or a selected log of firewood. The wood should be dry and it is advisable for the beginner to avoid the hard woods.

Our tools are a chisel, a rasp, a file and sandpaper for the final polish.

As a general principle, we should remove as little as possible from the piece of wood with which we start. We can often tell from the shape and structure of the block the kind of 'touch-form' that lies hidden within it. The term 'touch-form' denotes a shape that we enjoy touching, handling and moving about.

Before work starts, a very rough idea is decided on as to the general shape and character of the object we are going to fashion, that is, whether it is to be concave or convex or possibly have concave and convex surfaces alternating with one another. We then work down to the intended shape of the object using chisel, rasp and file. Sandpaper is used only after the surface is entirely even and smooth, for a final finishing. Anyone engaged in this form of play will soon understand how to work by means of his sense of touch; then the hand rather than the eye will take control as the object begins to assume shape. When the surface is completely smooth, the object should be soaked in a colourless hardening liquid, usually a cellulose preparation. After drying, it should be rubbed with fine sandpaper until only a faint shine remains. Heavy applications of varnish or similar preparations are out of harmony with the character of wood and tend to rob it of some of its natural charm. Figure 3: in the case of this touch-form the aim was an alternation of rough and smooth surfaces. (Steel brush.) Figures 4, 5, 7: in these, the process was begun by boring through the block. The shapes are largely determined by a certain balancing relationship between the size of the hole and the outward shape of the object.

9

3 S Ash

4 S Packing-wood

5 S Bongossi

6 S Macassar

7 S Bongossi

8 S Walnut   9 C 12 Walnut

TOUCH-TOYS

Where sculptural forms are concerned, lighting is a subsidiary but none the less indispensible means of achiev-ing a desired effect. Touch-forms, however, remain effective without any lighting at all, since their form can be fully understood by the sense of touch alone. We can observe this in the reactions of the blind. But in the case of those who can see, the sense of touch is largely undeveloped; far too little is done to foster it even when dealing with children. Among the vast numbers of toys that industry puts on the market, only a few make any appeal to this sense of touch, only a few are so shaped that a child would want to hold them because of their shape alone, only a few lie agreeably in the hand. Perhaps the examples shown here will encourage those who study them to make some really good touch-toys out of blocks of wood. No special kinds of wood are needed. The waste from any carpenter's shop will provide ample material.

When setting ourselves a task, and this applies no matter what kind of form we have in mind, we can approach it in one of two ways. We can pick out a block of wood because it roughly corresponds in shape and structure to a form already present in our imagination, or we can cut a block of wood down to the dimensions we require for a specific purpose. Beginners are advised to start with simple animal forms such as birds or fish.

11

10 S Walnut Elm

11 S Larch

12 S Larch

13 S Walnut   14 S Lime

We should make it a rule never to cut more from a block than is absolutely necessary to shape the required form. The important thing is to concentrate on the main lines of the figure and not get lost in a mass of detail. This is the reason for reducing to a minimum what we cut away from the block. In the examples shown, this principle was observed and real feeling was shown for the character of the woods selected. As a result, the essential forms of the subjects chosen emerged in a much more pronounced fashion than they do in representations of animals that have every detail of the bodily structure meticulously elaborated. Such detailed objects are produced by industry in vast quantities, but they leave no room for the free exercise of the child's imagination, and therefore are quite unsuitable for any kind of creative play.

In many of the examples shown we can see the extent to which the shape of the figure and the character of the wood have been allowed to interact.

Figure 12: length 12 in.

Figure 14: bold simple lines. Height 12 in. Burnt lime.

15 C 14 Scotch Pine

16 S Walnut

17 C 13 Scotch Pine

18 C 14 Scotch Pine

19 S Elm

20 S Scotch Pine

41 C 11 C 11 C 10

42 C 13 C 10 C 13

43 C 14

Plate I

21 S Lime

22 S

23 S Larch

Figure 21: darkened by burning in a gas flame and afterwards rubbed with a cloth. Cuts with a knife gave a lively quality to the surface.

Figure 22: fashioned from a bent twig.

Figure 23: the finished figure was treated with a sandblast. Increased emphasis was thus given to the structure of the larchwood.

24 S Alder

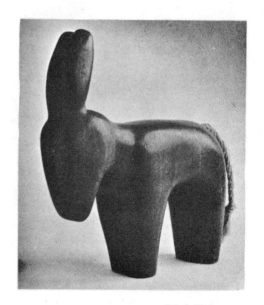

25 S Makore

26 C 14 Scotch Pine

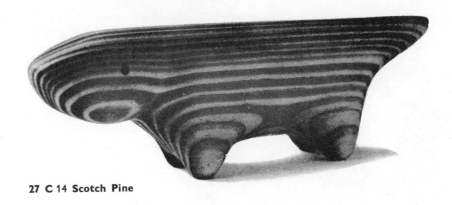

27 C 14 Scotch Pine

28 S Walnut

Figures 26, 27: considerable harmony was achieved between the shape of the figure and the grain of the wood.

Figure 28: length 16 in.

29 I Lime

30 I

Figure 29: carved out of limewood and burnt over a gas flame. Part of the figure was polished, producing an interesting contrast between lighter and darker surfaces. The ears were inserted.

20

31 C 14 Scotch Pine

Figure 31: the grain of the wood, which successfully combines with the general shape of the figure, was emphasized by slight burning. A soldering lamp was used for this.

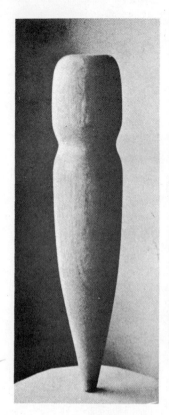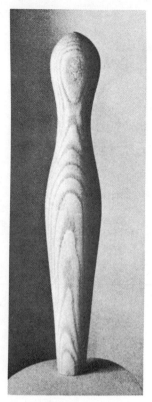

| 32 S Beech | 33 S Beech | 34 S S Ash | 35 C 15 Larch |

DOLLS

The illustrations show a systematic series of developments leading from a dibble to a skittle and thence to a doll. To the toy-maker who takes a serious view of his pedagogic function, the doll presents special problems. It must be well-shaped and of good material, it must stimulate the child's imagination, it should be easy to hold and should not be too heavy.

The examples shown contrast sharply with the typical elaborately modelled 'sweet' doll with real hair and eyes that can open and close. However, the unpretentious type of doll illustrated here exercises a mysterious influence on children. To a certain extent these dolls represent primal forms that a child's imagination can endow in any way it pleases.

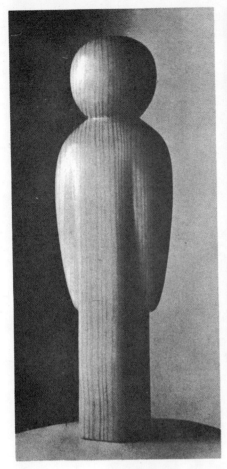

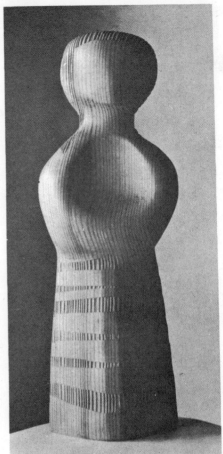

36 S Scotch Pine   37 S Scotch Pine   38 S Scotch Pine

Figures 32, 33: dibbles with soft transitions and clearly defined parts.

The forms of a dibble and a skittle are largely determined by their functions.

When carved wooden shapes are painted, the number of colours should be strictly limited and applied as sparingly as possible.

Figure 39: effective use of contrasts between surface with line, coloured surface and plain wooden surface.

Figures 41, 42 (facing page 16): typical expressions of a child's mind. Made with saw, rasp and file from thick pieces of rounded wood or from fence pickets.

Figure 43 (facing page 16): mature work of a fourteen-year-old. Paint applied sparingly and few colours used.

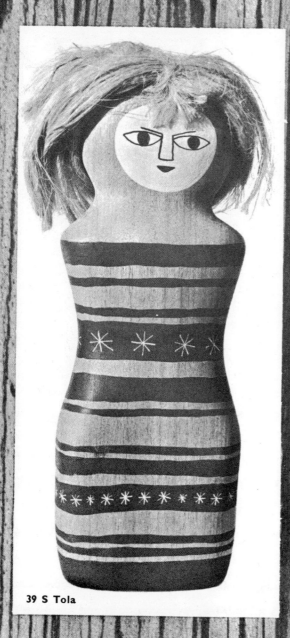

39 S Tola

40 S Tola

44 S Lime   45 S Lime   46 S Lime

To conclude our observations on dolls, here are a few words about hand-puppets. The expressiveness of these depends primarily on the shape of the head. The more boldly modelled the features of such a head are, the greater is the possibility of using light and shade to bring about changes in expression during stage perform-ances. Soft woods, such as lime or elm, are best for Punch and Judy heads. Heads made of papier mâché or other synthetic material invariably disappoint anyone who has ever carved a head of wood and used it in a puppet theatre.

47 C 13 Scotch Pine

ANIMALS MADE OUT OF BLOCKS AND ROUND PIECES OF WOOD

In examples 47-51, the aim of the exercise was to make animals by fitting separate pieces of wood together. Head and body were to be connected by means of a rod fitted into a borehole. The head was to be so affixed that it could be turned around. The legs were to consist of round pieces of wood which fitted into bore-holes and were glued to the body.

Figure 47: head and ears can be turned around. Head, ears and body are of pine. The legs are round pieces of beechwood. The pine was burnt with a soldering lamp to bring out the grain. The beechwood was subjected to more intense burning and no grain structure is visible.

Figure 48: head and body are of Scotch pine, the horns and legs are made from round pieces of beechwood.

Figure 49: made of turned lime and beech. Head and ears are movable. The ears are layered (see chapter on layering).

48 C 15 Scotch Pine

49 S Scotch Pine

50 S Scotch Pine

51 S Scotch Pine

Figures 50, 51: made of turned and burnt pine. The rhinoceros was rubbed with a cloth. The head of the hippopotamus was turned on a lathe and carved.

Figure 52: a large toy made from a single piece of wood hollowed out like a bowl. It runs on four eccentrically placed wheels and is large enough for a small child to sit upon. Although it is grotesque in its movements, this toy is well balanced in shape, and almost indestructible.

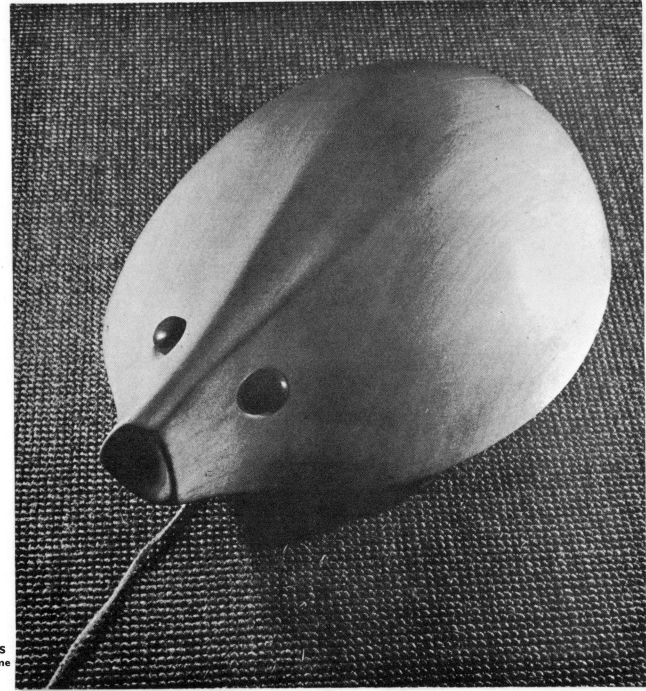

52 S
Lime

29

53 S Gaboon

54 S Lime Plum

55 S Oak

MAKING HOLLOW OBJECTS OUT OF A WOODEN BLOCK

The fashioning of hollow objects requires particular care. Using a hollow chisel and without any preliminary marking out, we start off by hollowing out a cavity in a block that corresponds to the proposed dimensions of our bowl. The wall of the cavity must be symmetrical all around and its contour gentle in line. Sharp tools are necessary for this work. Any testing of the cavity should be done by touch. Sandpaper should be used only after all unevenness has been removed from the wall. When the inner shape is complete, the outer shape should be decided on. The keynote of the design should be severity and should avoid any exaggerated modernism. Pear and cherry wood are particularly suitable materials, but seasoned oak and ash are also excellent for carving.

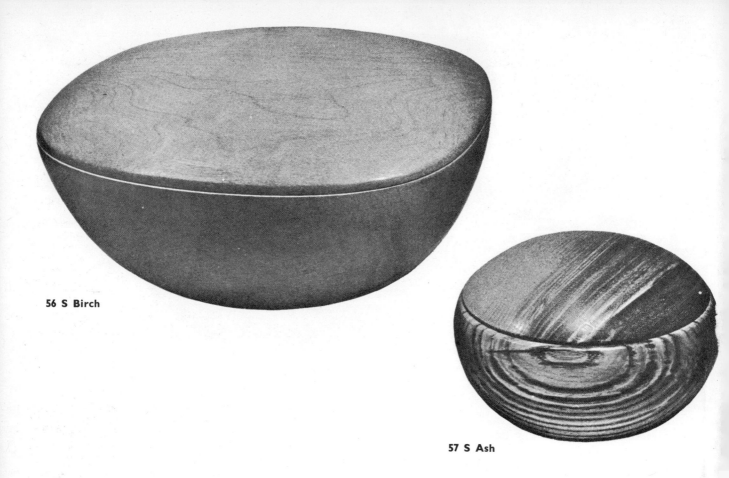

56 S Birch

57 S Ash

Figure 53: bowl with edge of varying width.

Figure 54: spoons should show a gentle transition from the internal to the external form.

Figure 55: hand-carved bowl treated with sandblast.

Figure 56: hand-carved bowl with lid. Fitting the lid requires a certain amount of experience.

Figure 58: hand-carved. Ash.

When objects are shaped on the lathe, the mark of the maker's personality is less apparent. Nevertheless the use of the lathe for hollowing helps to cultivate the sense of form.

Figure 57: shaped on the lathe.

Figure 59: birch bowl and elm mug. Turned.

58 S

59 S

Plate II

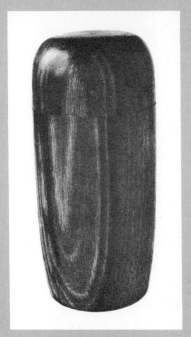

60 S Walnut

61 S Walnut

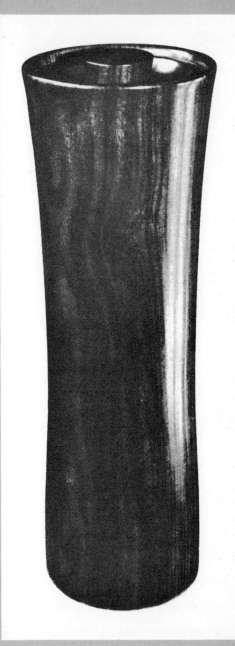

Figure 62: height 14 in.

62 I Cocobola

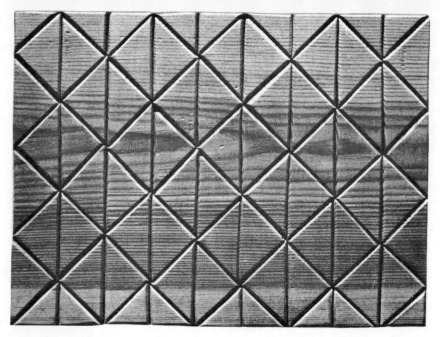

63 S

Starting with a Board

A board is the most familiar form of timber. And with few exceptions, the suggestions in the next twenty-eight pages embody ideas that can be carried out on a board, using only simple tools. The most important of these tools is the fret-saw. Although its past role in the disfigurement of so many homes has brought it into undeserved disrepute, the fret saw, if it is used with anything like a real feeling for design, has limitless possibilities. Moreover, if suitable blades are used, fairly thick boards can be cut with it.

34

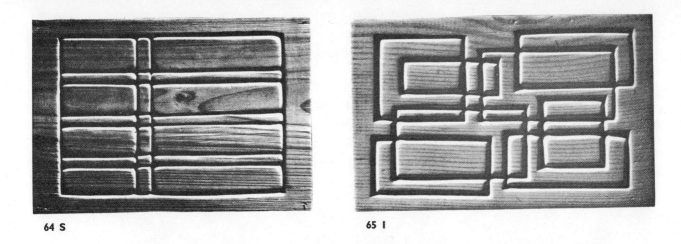

64 S

65 I

66 I

LINE RELIEFS

Figure 63: Scotch pine board cut into triangles with a fret saw. The cuts were broken through with a file to separate the parts. The parts were then glued to a plywood or fibre-board base in their original positions.

Figure 64: the surface of the wood was divided into rectangles which do not interesect.

67 I

68 I

69 C 13

70 I

71 S

72 I

Figures 65, 66: Again the surface of the wood was given a pattern of rectangles. In this case the rectangles intersect. The Scotch pine boards shown here are about 2/5 in. thick.

Figures 67-70: figures in line-relief.

Figure 69: a piece of plywood cut in the shape of a leaf was divided with a fret-saw. The parts were cleanly separated with a file, arranged at some distance from one another, and then glued to a wooden surface.

Figure 70: here the grain of the wood formed part of the design.

Figures 71-73: transition from line-relief to extended surface-relief. In the latter, the separate parts are fitted on the base in such a way that the grain of each part runs crosswise to the grain of the adjacent area.

Figure 73: here the direction of the grain is alternated to produce a chess-board effect.

73 S

74 S

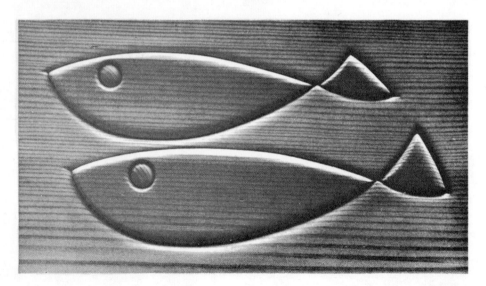

75 I

Figures 74, 75: by vigorously rubbing away the edges of the figures and giving some of them slight support from below, we achieve a sculptural effect as distinct from linear treatment.

38

 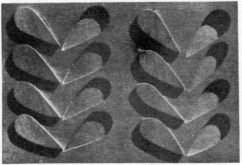 

76 S   77 S   78 S

EXTENDED SURFACE RELIEFS

Figures are cut out of a board or sheet of plywood, and placed on uncut areas of the same board and glued down. The board or piece of plywood is then glued to a second board or plywood sheet. The general plan determines the shape and number of the various figures and their arrangement. Nothing must be added or taken away. Such exercises bring out very clearly the character of this kind of play. There is plenty of scope for the imagination. In addition, although the various cut-out figures are moved about in what is essentially a spirit of play, this activity provides a good grounding in the principles of design that govern a two-dimensional layout.

In this kind of work it is well to limit the variety of figures that make up the patterns.

Figure 77: simple alignment of identical shapes of varying size.

Figure 78: dispersal of identical shapes of varying size. These shapes suggest nature motifs. The cut-outs have simply been turned over.

79 S

80 S

81 S

82 S

83 S

The illustrations on these pages give some concept of the great variety of ideas that can be employed. Tracing out the way in which the reliefs were devised is something of a game in itself. Nothing was added, nor was anything removed in any of these exercises.

84 S

85 S

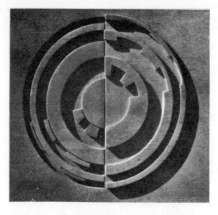

86 S

87 S

88 I

89 S

The examples shown here are particularly instructive because of the rhythmic relationship between the positive and negative forms. The procedure used is made exceptionally clear in Figure 88. The simple outline of a fish was cut out of the upper half of a plywood board. Then this board was glued on another plywood board. Small parts, such as eyes and scales, were sawed out of the positive fish figure and glued into the negative figure, now backed by the second board. The positive figure was reversed and glued to the lower half of the board.

Figure 89: positive and negative figures form a single design despite the fact that each is arranged differently.

90 I

91 I

92 I

93 I

Figures 90-93: the same procedure has been followed as in Figure 88.

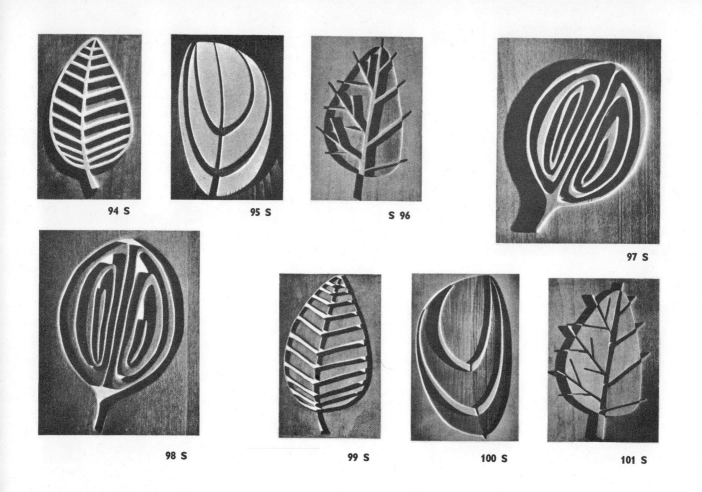

94 S 95 S S 96 97 S

98 S 99 S 100 S 101 S

Figures 94-110: variations on a leaf theme. In some cases either the cut-out surfaces or the under surfaces were stained.

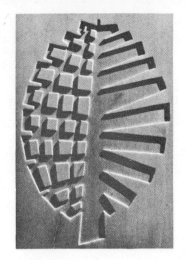

102 S

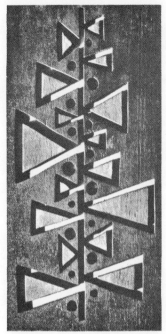

103 S

104 S

105 S

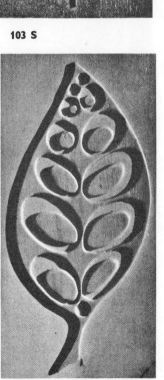

106 S

107 S

45

108 S

109 S

110 S

Figure 110: parts of the cut-out sections were stained. They were variously divided and arranged.

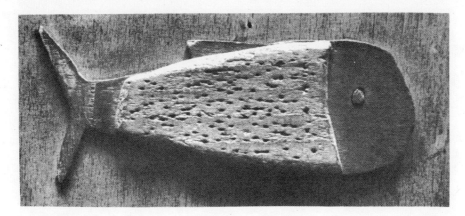

111 C 10

112 I

Figures 111, 112: cut-out figures glued to a wooden surface. Here a child's work can be compared with that of an adult.

113 S Pear-tree

PLASTIC TREATMENT OF A SURFACE BY CHIP-CARVING

Chip-carving, a method popular in the last century, is seldom used now. Items ornamented with the complicated geometical patterns formerly executed by this method are classed today as old-time horrors.

However, the examples shown here prove that if intelligently applied chip-carving need not offend our modern sense of form.

Figure 113: despite the strict alignment of negative and positive elements, these geometrical figures, carved out of limewood with a chipping tool, impart a lively rhythm to this surface.

Figures 114, 115: two ways of solving the same problem. It was decided that three square spaces should be left untouched. The rest of the surface could be treated in any way the worker pleased.

114 S Lime

115 S Lime

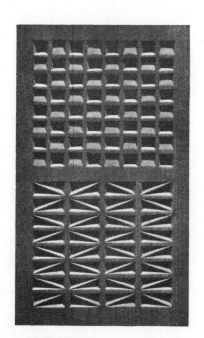

116 S Lime

117 S Lime

49

118 S Lime

119 S Maple

Figure 118: a novel conception of chip-carving which imparts a strong rhythmical expression to the work.

Figure 119: chip-carving used in the production of a set of dominoes, which, incidentally, can be used by the blind.

50

Figure 120: the character of the larchwood has been sharply emphasized by the use of a sandblast. As a result, the grain of the wood combines with the geometrical forms to give an effect of strong relief.

120 S Larch

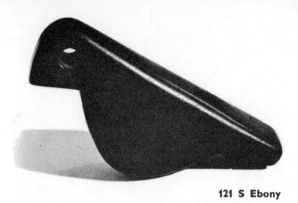

121 S Ebony

122 S

123 S Lime Gaboon

CUTTING ANIMALS OUT OF A BOARD

It is best to make a template of the general design first. Cut the silhouette out of cardboard with a pair of scissors without making any preliminary drawing. In this way you will avoid getting lost in petty detail. A fret-saw can be used on soft wood, a bow-saw on hard wood.

Figure 123: surface enlivened by inlays of differently coloured wood (borer, dowel-pin).

Figure 124: tail and mane made of hemp.

Figure 125: surface enlivened by small polished strips of veneer, glued on.

124 S Walnut

125 S Lime

53

126 S Lime

127 C 12 C 14 Scotch Pine

Figure 126: this figure was darkened by burning in a gas flame. Afterwards the head was lightly rubbed with sandpaper. The notches were made with a knife, and the holes with a nail.

Toys of this kind are suitable for production in quantity, and the following procedure is often used by home industry. A piece of wood is carved lengthwise so that a cross-section shows the silhouette of an animal. The wood is then cut into sections and these are finished off as required.

128 S Lime

129 S Beech

In all ages, negative reliefs have been used as moulds for shaping bread, butter, cakes and so forth. To make these, again the best method of procedure is to use a template for outlining the basic shape on the wood. The basic shape is hollowed out, in the manner of a bowl, to a depth of 1/8 in., then thoroughly polished. This step must be completed before the subsidiary elements of the design (lines, planes and so on) are chipped or chiselled out. The most suitable material is beechwood, 1/5 in. thick.

Figure 129: length of mould 20 in.

130 C 12

INLAY WORK

The simplest forms of inlay work are illustrated on pages 56-58.

Figures are cut out of a piece of plywood with a fret-saw. They are then stained and re-inserted. The whole is then glued to a base of plywood or fibre.

Before this work is attempted a design should be made. Then the required shapes should be cut out of sheets of coloured paper laid on top of one another, by means of scissors, knife or marquetry knife. After this, proceeding as usual in a spirit of playful experiment, we can try out a variety of different arrangements until we get a really satisfactory result. (A large variety of suggestions for decorative layouts of surfaces can be found in Creative Paper Design, the first volume of this series.) Transfer the design to the plywood by outlining the different cut-outs with a pencil. A simple water-stain is satisfactory for staining.

These preliminaries determine the character, size and arrangement of the various figures and the colours of the stains.

Flat-surface layouts with geometrical figures are illustrated on the opposite page.

Figure 132: a design made of cellophane pieces.

Figure 133: this design of intersecting rectangles was carried out by placing pieces of cardboard cross-wise and outlining them with a pencil.

Figure 134: this design was produced by cutting semi-circles out of paper strips. The clearly recognizable irregularities in the lines of the saw-cuts are typical of inlay work done with a fret-saw. The noticeable impress of the maker's personality lends a special charm to the work.

131 C 12

132 I

133 I

134 C 13

135 C 12

136 C 15

Figure 135, 136: Despite restriction to fewer forms, two individual and quite different solutions were found.

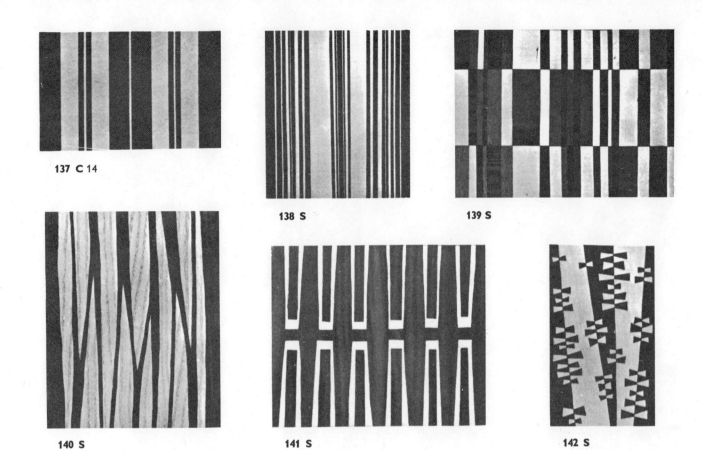

137 C 14

138 S

139 S

140 S

141 S

142 S

TARSIA WORK

Tarsia work is carried out by means of veneers. We must distinguish between processes requiring the use of a knife and those requiring the use of a saw; the knife is more suitable for straight-line patterns, the saw is better for curves. A knife was used in all the examples shown here. In tarsia work, too, it is advisable first to build up the design with pieces of coloured cardboard.

Figure 137: vertical division of a flat surface, the contrast being between light and dark and between narrow and broad. Pear and maple.

Figure 138: the pattern proceeds rhythmically from the centre towards the sides. Maple and Brazilian rosewood.

Figure 139: this design is marked by a noticeable severity. It consists of three horizontal bands divided into rectangles of equal height but varying breadth. Three different veneers were used: maple, walnut and Brazilian rosewood.

Figure 140: vertical arrangement with marked liveliness of line. Carried out with two veneers: ash and pear.

143 S

144 S

Figure 142: design formed by dividing a rectangular piece of paper. Trapezoid shapes were cut out of the sides of the strips and flapped over. Maple and Brazilian rosewood.

Figure 143: flat-surface layout using rectangular figures. The cuts were made with a knife. Four veneers were used: maple, pear, cherry and walnut.

Figure 144: layout of a flat surface with rounded figures lying one within the other. Cuts were made with a saw. Four veneers were used: ash, pear, walnut and cherry.

Technical hints on tarsia work will be found on page 78.

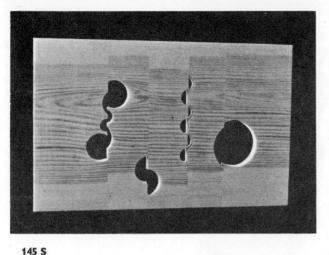

145 S

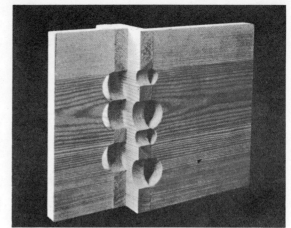

146 S

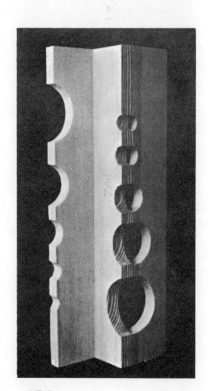

147 S

THREE-DIMENSIONAL STRUCTURES MADE FROM A BOARD

Holes of various sizes are made in a board with a centre-bit. The board is then cut into strips in such a manner that the line of some of the cuts passes through the center of the holes. The strips can then be so combined that the semicircular cuts are aligned with one another in various ways and stand in new relationships to each other as part of a single design.

Figure 145: two-dimensional combination.

Figures 146-148: three-dimensional combinations.

61

148 S

Layering

Earlier we saw how figures, among them actual representations of animals, could be made from a block of wood by removing parts of the block. Another method of producing sculptural shapes is by layering, a method by which layers of wood are glued one on top of the other. This is done until the desired shape of the object to be produced becomes crudely discernible. Of course at this stage the super-imposition of the different layers of wood creates a stepped effect and work must be done with rasp, file and sandpaper until the finished form emerges. This method of procedure enables us to use different thicknesses of wood—from veneer down to an actual plank. These differences in the thicknesses and character of woods are in themselves sufficient to ensure the possibility of a wide variety in design. In addition, through the use of a number of different woods, colour becomes a contributory element in the final effect. The actual technical procedure is illustrated in some detail in figures 149-151.

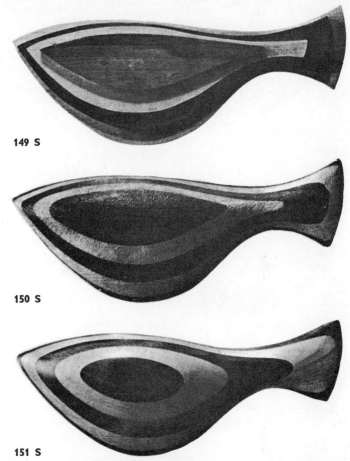

149 S

150 S

151 S

Figure 149: we start with a piece of board cut in the shape of a fish. This forms the central layer on both sides of which several other layers are glued. The outline of each additional layer is a fraction smaller than that of the one below it. At this stage the surface of the whole is still a series of steps leading from one layer to another. The effect is similar to the contours of a map.

Figure 150: the edges of the different layers have been filed down with a rasp, so that the steps leading from one layer to another have disappeared.

Figure 151: the finished article. The whole surface has been smoothed with a file and polished with sandpaper.

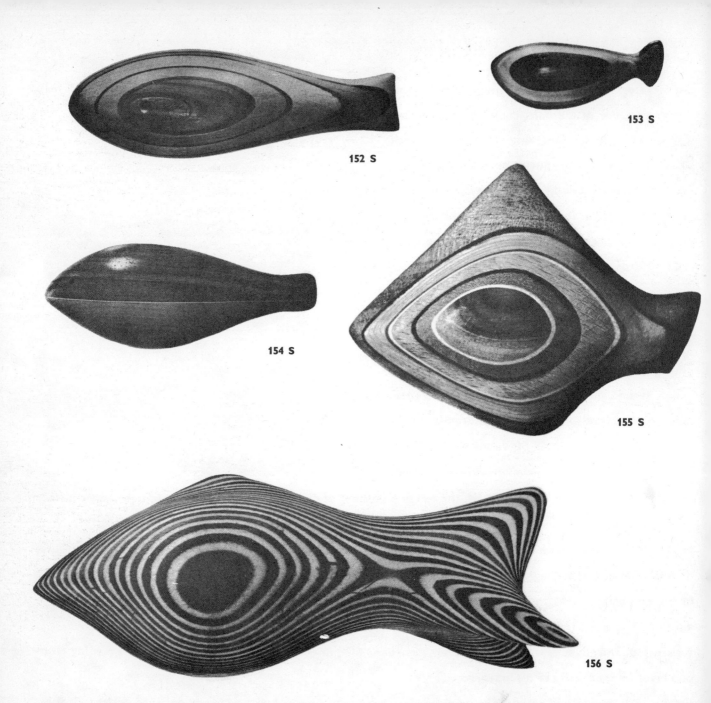

152 S

153 S

154 S

155 S

156 S

64

172 I

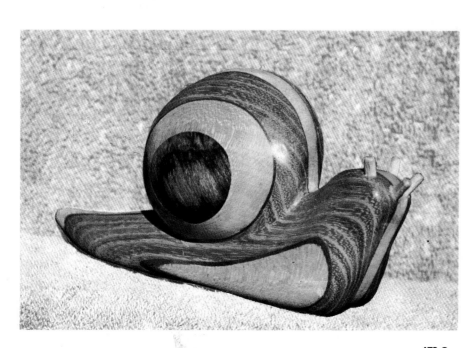

173 S

Plate III

157 I

158 I

159 S

160 S

Figure 154: two solid pieces of wood have been used together with veneers. Walnut, cherry and maple.

Figure 156: Layer-work consisting entirely of veneers.

Figure 160: layered from beech-wood board. The comb and the beak are part of the middle section.

161 S

162 C 14

Figure 161: First a block was made by glueing various woods together. The figure was then sawed out of the block and given its final shape by filing.

Figure 162: the work of a child, clearly showing a strong feeling for form. The head and neck are made from a thick middle layer.

Figure 163: pine, cherry and beech plywood.

Figure 164: beech, oak, gaboon and pear veneers.

Figure 165: Layers of solid wood and veneers. Concentration on main line of figure. Length 8 in.

163 C 12

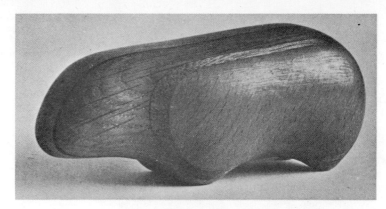

164 C 13

165 I

166 C 14

Figure 166: layers made of carpenter's waste and odd bits of plywood, as we can see from the fact that the layering goes both lengthwise and crosswise. The legs are part of the outer layer.

167 S

Figure 167: the effectiveness of this figure is largely due to the contrasts between narrowness and width, and between light and dark colours; this effect is produced by using thick pieces of wood and veneers. Cherry and maple veneer.

168 C 8

Figure 168: this elephant, monumental in its effect, is the work of an eight-year-old child. Made of layers of wood cut out with a fret-saw, then glued together. The figure was painted blue. Eyes and teeth are inset. The work shows a child's strong inborn sense of form. Two thirds of actual size.

169 I

170 I

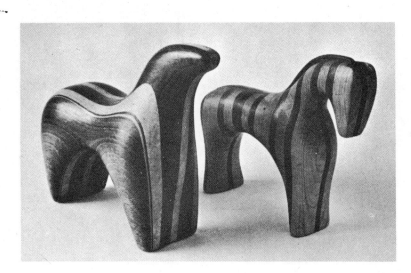

171 S

Figure 169: beech and walnut.

Figure 170: crosswise layering of a number of woods: walnut, maple, ash and cherry.

Figure 171: the figure on the right is layered both lengthwise and crosswise. Walnut and maple, ash and walnut.

174 S

175 S

Figure 172 (facing page 64): pine, beech, birch plywood and walnut veneer.

Figure 173 (facing page 64): acacia, beech and walnut.

Figure 174: blocks consisting of glued layers were turned on the lathe. The legs were bored in. Maple and walnut.

Figure 175: legs and tusks have been inserted. Gaboon and fir, stained.

BUILDING UP HOLLOW OBJECTS IN LAYERS

As in the fashioning of solid figures, layering can also be used in building up hollow objects.

Using woods of varying thickness (boards, plywood, veneers), we begin by sawing out rings and frames which are then glued together. Sides are neatly filed and smoothed, first inside, then out. The bottom is also attached with glue. It is best to groove the lid. The effect can be heightened by using a number of differently coloured woods.

Figure 176: this shows the pleasing effect of a very slight curve. The boxes on the left are of maple with pear veneer, the one on the right is of beech, cherry, acacia and pear veneers.

Figure 177: the box on the left is built up of oak boards with the pattern of the grain alternating in direction. The oak is interleaved with maple veneer. The receptacle on the right is of maple, ash, pear and cherry.

Figure 178: the oval receptacles are of plum with maple and Brazilian rosewood veneers.

177 I · S

178 S

179 C 14

180 C 14

181 I

182 S

183 S

HOLLOW OBJECTS TURNED ON THE LATHE

A number of different woods are layered and glued together to form a block. The hollow shape is then produced by the ordinary processes of turnery.

Figure 183: vessels of cherry and maple shaped on the lathe.

Figures 179, 180: receptacles which show a child's innate power of formal self-expression. The receptacle on the left is made of pine board and beech plywood, that on the right of gaboon plywood.

Figure 181: boats made of a variety of woods.

Figure 182: a layered Noah's Ark on wheels. Cherry, maple, Scotch pine. Length 20 in.

184 S

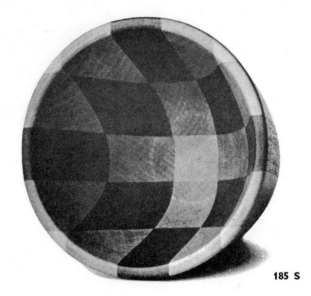

185 S

Figure 184: rectangular bars made from different kinds of wood were glued together to form a block. The mug was then formed on a lathe, working in the direction of the grain. Beech, maple, African pear.

HOLLOW OBJECTS MADE OF VENEER

New types of glue now enable us to make certain combinations of woods which formerly were either impossible or very difficult to achieve. Products like Bostik are extraordinarily quick-drying; wooden surfaces treated with them only need to be pressed together once to form an entirely firm junction. This opens up creative possibilities that are altogether new. Among other things, our experiments have led to the fashioning of hollow objects made entirely of veneers. To do this, we begin by winding a veneer around a mould, which may consist of a cardboard roll, a bottle, or a round piece of wood. The grain must follow the line of the mould

186 S

lengthwise. One end of the veneer is laid on top of the other, the edges having been trimmed so that an absolutely tight fit is secured. Then a piece of Cellophane is glued over the joint so that we get a cylinder of veneer that can be pushed up and down along the mould. After this, we can glue layer after layer of veneer around the original cylinder, always being sure to rub each layer firmly with a hammer before applying the next one. However, care must be taken to ensure that the different joins do not lie on top of one another. The more layers we glue on, the firmer the shape will become. We thus end up with a firmly walled cylinder for which we can supply a bottom and a lid.

The mould can also be rectangular with rounded corners, or it can be oval, or have a number of concave sides. A block of wood can be cut to the desired shape.

Considerable freedom can be exercised in the treatment of the surface. It can be enlivened by tarsia work or by reliefs cut out of veneer.

Figure 186: two cylinders were formed around the mould, one over the other, producing a narrower and a wider one. The narrower one constitutes the inside of the box. The wider one has been divided and forms the outer side of the lower portion and the side of the lid. Pear and walnut.

Figure 187: a cylindrical box with alternations of light and dark veneer. The layering is clearly recognizable. The line of the surface has been broken by rings turned on the lathe.

187 S Maple, Brazilian Rosewood Veneer

TECHNICAL HINTS FOR THE MAKING OF TARSIAS

The veneers selected for the tarsia work are placed one on top of the other in layers and fastened together with soluble lime (bone-glue). It is advisable to place a piece of paper between the different layers of veneer to prevent the wood from splitting when it is cut. After the design has been traced on the top layer of veneer, the various figures are cut out with a knife, or with a fret-saw fitted with only the finest blade. If these glued figures are placed in warm water, the various layers will come apart and so give us the same number of pieces, repeating each particular figure, as there are layers of veneer. These can be dried between sheets of blotting paper. Now we are ready to re-create the original pattern. This will not be difficult, even though at this point we work with a variety of identically shaped pieces of veneer which we can combine as we please. After completing the pattern, the whole surface is covered with adhesive strips, then glued, wood downward, to a plywood base. This is then placed between two boards, generously padded with newspaper, until the glue has set. Then the adhesive is moistened and removed with a broad punch, after which the surface is smoothed with scraper and sandpaper. The surface is then treated with cellulose in the usual way.

Figures 188, 189 (facing page 80): surfaces decorated with tarsia work. In the case of the low oval receptacle, pieces of veneer have been used to produce a relief effect. Maple, cherry and maple, cherry and pear. Maple and walnut, maple, pear, cherry and walnut.

190 S

Figure 190: veneer cut into the shape of a net and glued over a receptacle. Oak and walnut veneer.

191 C 11 C 10 C 11

192 C 11 C 11

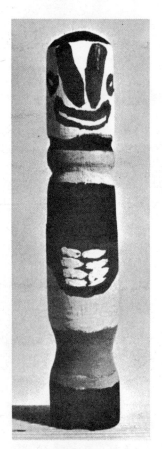

193 C 12

194 C 12 C 13

188 S

189 S

Plate IV

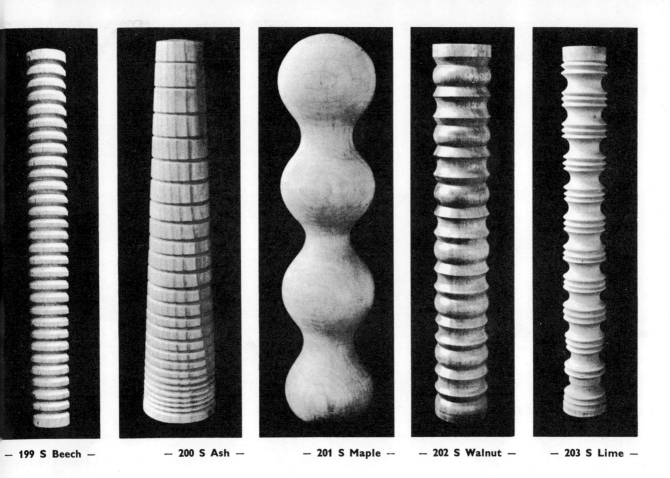

| — 199 S Beech — | — 200 S Ash — | — 201 S Maple — | — 202 S Walnut — | — 203 S Lime — |

USING THE LATHE TO FASHION FORMS FROM ROUNDED WOOD

A few examples are enough to show how the lathe can be used to solve certain simple problems of design. The pleasing effect of these pieces of turned wood is due to economy in the selection of forms.

Figure 199: simple circular notches evenly spaced.

Figure 200: change of direction in the movement of the line. Regular increases in size of the intervals between the lines.

Figure 201: indentations with soft transitions.

Figures 202, 203: severe alignment of concave and convex rings.

— 195 C 11 —

— 196 C 13 C 13 —

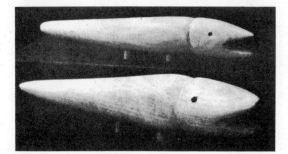

— 197 C 12 C 13 —

— 198 C 11 C 14 —

Starting with a Round Piece of Wood or with a Wooden Strip

MAKING TOYS FROM A ROUND PIECE OF WOOD

A round piece of wood is cut into pieces and the pieces are shaped with a carving tool, rasp and file. Th

practice is to define, in advance, the general character of the job, deciding on size, shape, colour and th

to be employed.

The examples shown here were all made from a broom-stick.

Figures 191, 192: this exercise consisted of first shaping a piece of wood in the form of a skittle, then pai

using very few colours. The addition of bast and feathers was permitted for purposes of subsidiary deco

Figure 193: the painting of this figure shows a sure instinct for colour and is admirably adapted to the

shape.

Figure 194: figure fashioned with rasp, file and knife and painted.

Figure 195: fashioned with rasp and file from short pieces of wood.

Figures 196-198: little rounded pieces of wood were bored in to serve as legs. Few other parts were adde

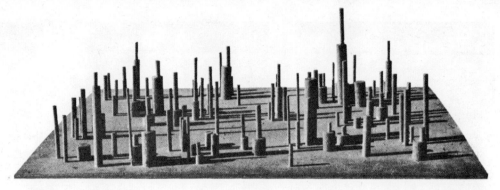

204 S

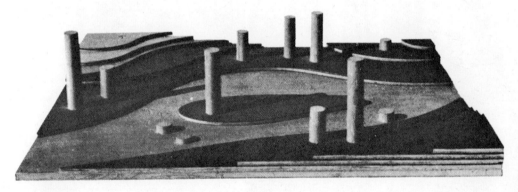

205 S

CONSTRUCTIVE BUILDING WITH WOODEN RODS

Figure 204: rods of varying length and thickness were fitted on a base-plate and given a clearly discernible order with rhythmic balance.

Figure 205: here the problem was to arrange rods of equal thickness but of varying length on a base to be built up in relief by layering.

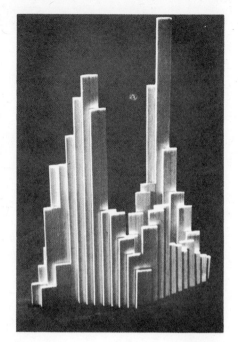

206 I

207 I

208 S

CONSTRUCTIVE BUILDING WITH WOODEN STRIPS

A strip of wood is cut into sections which form the constructional elements for the exercise. The aim is to create three dimensional structures by glueing the sections together with some kind of quick-drying glue.

Figures 206-208: various solutions of the above problem in which strips of varying length are used.

Figures 209-211: three further solutions in which the small wooden strips are of equal size and are so arranged that the resulting structure stands on four feet.

Figure 212: one design horizontally imposed on a second. The two designs are identical, though differing in scale.

209 I

210 S

211 S

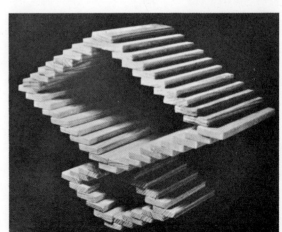

212 C 13

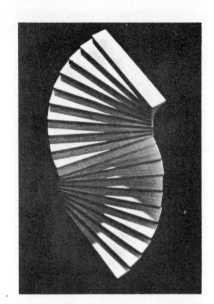

214 I

213 C 14

215 C 14

Figures 213-215: three further solutions. Here the wooden strips are again of equal size and combined into a winding pattern. A strong plastic effect is achieved through fluid transitions.

216 I

217 I

218 S

Figures 216, 217: various ways of carrying out spiral exercises. All the wooden strips had to be of equal size.

Figure 218: freely constructed three-dimensional design. Again, the strips had to be of equal size.

219 S   220 S   221 S

Constructional Sets, Joining Pieces of Wood, Play Materials

Devising constructional or building sets with pieces that fit into one another is a very rewarding occupation. The essential features can be easily recognized in the illustrations, so that only few explanatory remarks are needed.

Figure 219: a three-dimensional construction built up out of rectangular strips of plywood of varying size. These fit into one another by means of slits made with a saw.

Figure 220: construction built up of two kinds of building elements made to fit into one another.

Figure 221: construction in which only a single type of building element has been used.

Figure 222: constructional set in which the pieces fit together by means of slots and pins. The sides of the box hold together by means of interlocking prongs. The lid consists of wooden blocks made of three different woods glued together.

Figure 223: building elements consisting of a number of discs turned on the lathe and divided in various ways.

222 S

223 S

224 S

225 S

Figures 224, 225: constructional set. The flat
pieces are notched so they can be fitted into
each other or onto the rods. The box is in the
form of a wagon with removable sides.

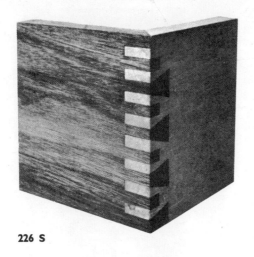

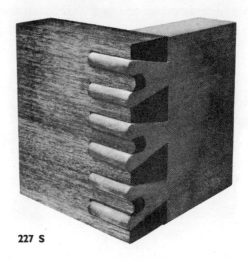

226 S

227 S

JOINING PIECES OF WOOD TOGETHER

When pieces of wood are joined together, the success of the operation is usually evaluated in terms of technical efficiency alone. The accompanying illustrations show that the joining can also play an important part in the design of the form.

A great number of ideas have been incorporated in the examples shown and it is obvious that the demands made on the workers' inventive powers were considerable.

Figures 226, 227: two examples of wood firmly joined in a strictly traditional manner. The use of different kinds of wood emphasises the beauty of the device employed.

The wooden shapes on page 92 can be joined and separated again. The illustrations show the both pieces separate and partly fitted together.

Figures 228, 229: fashioned by saw and chisel from a rectangular wooden block.

Figures 230, 231: combinations of rectangular wooden blocks and circular rods. Blocks and rods have been glued together.

Figures 232, 233: two round wooden bars equipped with transversely interlocking flanges.

Figures 234, 235: here twenty-five tenons taper into one another. Fashioned with chisel and saw.

It is easy to see these methods of joining pieces of wood have, among other things, a practical value, for example, in the making of furniture.

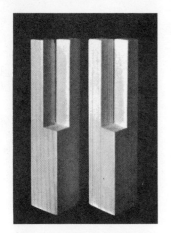

228 S

229 S

233 S

234 S

230 S

232 S

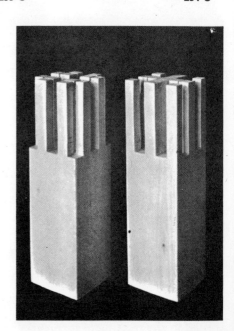

235 S

231 S

236 S

237 S

MACHINES FOR PLAY

Play that involves the construction of a whole out of parts leads to the construction of machines that can be used in play. The machines depicted here have not been built according to a previously devised plan. The initial idea behind them has simply been that of some specific function, such as the production of wave motion, or the effects of leverage. Once begun, building proceeded as experimental play until a functioning machine came into being. The object was not to invent a machine with any specific rational and utilitarian purpose. The aim was simply the joy of creation. The value and significance of these machines lies in the contribution they make to basic education, in the demands they make on imaginative and inventive powers and in their capacity to mobilize those powers. One might add that the laws of mechanics and certain rhythmic sequences of motion are far more vividly communicated in this way than would be the case with even the best theoretical instruction.

93

238 S

239 S

240 S

241 S

Figure 236: machine with lever transmission.

Figure 237: machine embodying the principle of the rammer.

Figure 238: adjustable hammer apparatus.

Figure 242: the horizontal cog-wheel is fitted loosely on a firm vertical axis. The two discs with holes in them are firmly attached to this axis. The only movable parts are, therefore, the two cog-wheels and the circular rods, which have been loosely fitted into the guide holes. When the machine revolves, the inclined plane, which has been affixed to the horizontal cog-wheel in the form of a spiral, causes the loose rods to be pushed gradually upwards. As these pass over the end of the inclined plane, they fall audibly and in rapid succession onto the flat surface of the cog-wheel and, as the cog-wheel continues to turn, are once more brought into contact with the inclined plane. Since the inclined plane is banked, it only touches the edge of the base of the rods, and so, as it moves, causes them to rotate around their own axes as they rise.

242 S

243 S

244 S

PLAY-DEVICES THAT PRODUCE SOUNDS

Figure 243: here is a structure on which balls can be dropped to produce sounds as they hit the wooden brackets. These little sounding brackets can be changed to produce different sequence of sounds, even to the point of producing an actual melody.

Figure 244: here the interchangeable sounding brackets are arranged on a box. This box produces increased resonance and serves as a receptable for additional balls.

Figure 239: by turning the wheel, small circular rods of varying lengths are plucked and produce sounds. The rods can be changed to produce different sound sequences. To hold the machine together the various parts are fitted into slots.